## Table of Contents

**Introduction ........................................................... 6**
*What is self-confidence? ................................................. 6*
*Why is it important to boost your self-confidence in specific areas? ................................................................ 8*
*How to boost your self-confidence in specific areas ........ 11*

**Chapter 1: The importance of boosting your self-confidence in specific areas ................................. 14**
*Self-confidence is essential for a happy and successful life ............................................................................. 14*
*When you have self-confidence, you are more likely to take risks, achieve your goals, and be happy with your life ......................................................................... 16*
*There are many things you can do to boost your self-confidence in specific areas ....................................... 18*

**Chapter 2: How to boost your self-confidence in specific areas ................................................... 21**
*Identify your self-confidence blocks ............................... 21*
*Challenge your negative thoughts ................................. 25*
*Focus on your strengths ................................................ 28*
*Set realistic goals ......................................................... 30*
*Take risks .................................................................... 32*
*Surround yourself with positive people ......................... 34*
*Practice positive self-talk ............................................. 36*

## Chapter 3: Boosting your self-confidence in your career ............................................................................. 38

*Set career goals ............................................. 38*
*Take on new challenges .................................... 40*
*Network with other professionals ....................... 42*
*Get involved in professional organizations ............ 44*
*Dress for success ............................................ 47*
*Be confident in your abilities ............................. 50*

## Chapter 4: Boosting your self-confidence in your relationships ........................................................ 54

*Be yourself .................................................... 54*
*Be honest and open with your partner ................. 57*
*Be supportive of your partner ............................ 60*
*Spend quality time together .............................. 63*
*Go on dates ................................................... 66*
*Make each other laugh .................................... 69*

## Chapter 5: Boosting your self-confidence in your personal life ........................................................ 72

*Set personal goals .......................................... 72*
*Take care of yourself ....................................... 76*
*Do things that make you happy ......................... 79*
*Spend time with loved ones .............................. 82*
*Give back to others ......................................... 85*
*Be grateful for what you have ........................... 88*

**Conclusion** .......................................................... **91**
  *The importance of boosting your self-confidence in*
  *specific areas*................................................................ *91*
  *How to boost your self-confidence in specific areas* ....... *94*
**Wordbook** ........................................................... **98**
**Supplementary Materials** ................................. **100**

# Introduction
## What is self-confidence?

Self-confidence can be defined as a belief in one's abilities, qualities, and judgment. It's the feeling of assurance and trust in oneself that allows us to take on challenges, pursue our goals, and cope with setbacks and failures.

Self-confidence is not a fixed trait, but rather a dynamic and flexible quality that can be developed and strengthened over time. It's also not an all-or-nothing proposition - we can be confident in some areas of our lives but not in others, and our level of confidence may fluctuate depending on the situation, our mood, or our past experiences.

Why is self-confidence important?

Self-confidence is a key ingredient for a fulfilling and successful life. Here are some of the reasons why:

1. Self-confidence enables us to take risks and pursue our goals. When we believe in ourselves, we're more likely to try new things, take on challenges, and persist in the face of obstacles. This can lead to personal growth, achievement, and a sense of fulfillment.

2. Self-confidence enhances our relationships. When we're confident in ourselves, we're more likely to be authentic, assertive, and communicative in our interactions

with others. This can help us build meaningful connections, resolve conflicts, and maintain healthy boundaries.

3. Self-confidence boosts our mental and physical well-being. When we're confident, we're less likely to experience anxiety, depression, or stress. We're also more likely to take care of ourselves, engage in healthy behaviors, and seek support when needed.

How can you boost your self-confidence?

If you're struggling with low self-confidence, don't worry - there are many things you can do to improve your self-esteem and self-belief. In this book, we'll explore some of the most effective strategies for boosting your self-confidence in specific areas of your life, such as your relationships, your career, or your health. By practicing these techniques and cultivating a growth mindset, you can unleash your potential and achieve greater happiness and success.

## Why is it important to boost your self-confidence in specific areas?

Sure, here's a possible draft for the "Why is it important to boost your self-confidence in specific areas?" section of the introduction:

Why is it important to boost your self-confidence in specific areas?

Self-confidence is a fundamental aspect of our mental and emotional well-being, and it impacts many areas of our lives. When we lack confidence, we may feel stuck, helpless, or insecure, which can hold us back from pursuing our goals and living up to our full potential. In this section, we'll explore some of the specific reasons why it's important to boost your self-confidence in specific areas of your life.

1. Boosting self-confidence can improve your performance.

When we believe in ourselves, we're more likely to perform well in the tasks we undertake. Self-confidence can help us approach challenges with a positive attitude, make better decisions, and stay focused on our goals. For example, if you're trying to advance your career, having confidence in your abilities can help you take on new responsibilities, speak up in meetings, and network with colleagues.

2. Boosting self-confidence can improve your relationships.

Self-confidence can also impact our relationships with others. When we feel good about ourselves, we're more likely to be assertive, communicate effectively, and set boundaries. This can help us build healthier relationships, resolve conflicts, and avoid getting stuck in unfulfilling or toxic dynamics. For example, if you're trying to improve your romantic relationships, having confidence in yourself can help you express your needs, listen empathetically to your partner, and enjoy intimacy.

3. Boosting self-confidence can improve your mental health.

Low self-confidence can contribute to a range of mental health issues, such as anxiety, depression, and low self-esteem. By boosting your self-confidence, you can improve your mental health and well-being, and reduce your risk of developing these conditions. For example, if you're struggling with anxiety, working on building your confidence can help you face your fears, challenge negative thoughts, and develop a more positive outlook.

4. Boosting self-confidence can improve your overall quality of life.

Ultimately, boosting your self-confidence can improve your overall quality of life. When you feel good about yourself and your abilities, you're more likely to enjoy your life, pursue your passions, and achieve your dreams. You'll be less likely to feel stuck or limited by your fears and insecurities, and more likely to embrace new opportunities and experiences.

In the following chapters, we'll explore specific strategies and techniques for boosting your self-confidence in specific areas of your life, such as your career, your relationships, and your personal life. By practicing these techniques and cultivating a growth mindset, you can unleash your potential and achieve greater happiness and success.

**How to boost your self-confidence in specific areas**

Boosting your self-confidence can be a challenging process, but it's a worthwhile investment in yourself and your future. In this section, we'll explore some of the key strategies and techniques for boosting your self-confidence in specific areas of your life.

1. Identify your self-confidence blocks

The first step to boosting your self-confidence is to identify the factors that are holding you back. These may include negative self-talk, past experiences of failure or rejection, or limiting beliefs about yourself and your abilities. By acknowledging these blocks and challenging them, you can start to shift your mindset and build a more positive and empowering self-image.

2. Challenge your negative thoughts

One of the most common blocks to self-confidence is negative self-talk. We all have a critical inner voice that can undermine our self-esteem and hold us back. To overcome this, you can practice challenging your negative thoughts with more balanced and realistic ones. For example, if you catch yourself thinking "I'm not good enough" or "I'll never succeed," you can try reframing those thoughts as "I have skills and strengths that I can build on" or "I can learn from my mistakes and improve over time."

3. Focus on your strengths

Another way to boost your self-confidence is to focus on your strengths and accomplishments. By recognizing what you're good at and what you've achieved, you can build a sense of pride and confidence in yourself. You can do this by making a list of your strengths and achievements, or by seeking feedback and recognition from others.

4. Set realistic goals

Setting goals that are challenging but achievable is another important aspect of boosting your self-confidence. When we have a clear sense of direction and purpose, we're more likely to feel motivated and confident in pursuing our goals. It's important to set goals that are specific, measurable, and time-bound, and to break them down into smaller steps that you can take action on.

5. Take risks

Stepping outside of your comfort zone and taking risks is another powerful way to build self-confidence. When we challenge ourselves and try new things, we expand our skills and abilities, and learn that we're capable of more than we thought. This can help us overcome our fears and insecurities, and build a sense of resilience and self-assurance.

6. Surround yourself with positive people

The people we surround ourselves with can have a big impact on our self-confidence. By seeking out positive and supportive people who believe in us and encourage us, we can build a stronger sense of self-worth and confidence. On the other hand, being around negative or critical people can undermine our self-esteem and make it harder to build confidence.

7. Practice positive self-talk

Finally, practicing positive self-talk is a key strategy for boosting self-confidence. By cultivating a more positive and compassionate inner dialogue, we can build a stronger sense of self-esteem and self-acceptance. This can involve using affirmations, visualizations, or other techniques to focus on our strengths and potential, and to counteract negative self-talk.

In the following chapters, we'll explore how to apply these strategies to specific areas of your life, such as your career, your relationships, and your personal life. By practicing these techniques and cultivating a growth mindset, you can unleash your potential and achieve greater happiness and success.

# Chapter 1: The importance of boosting your self-confidence in specific areas

## Self-confidence is essential for a happy and successful life

Self-confidence is an essential element for leading a happy and successful life. It is the foundation of your mental and emotional well-being and enables you to face and overcome the various challenges that life presents.

When you have self-confidence, you have an inner belief in yourself and your abilities, which allows you to pursue your goals and ambitions with conviction. Self-confidence gives you the courage to take risks, and you become more willing to try new things, explore new opportunities and take on challenges that may have seemed daunting or impossible before.

Having self-confidence also enables you to have a positive outlook on life. You tend to focus more on the opportunities rather than the obstacles and setbacks. You become more resilient and adaptable to change, and you are better equipped to cope with the ups and downs of life.

Self-confidence is also crucial for maintaining healthy relationships. When you believe in yourself, you are better equipped to handle conflicts and communicate more effectively with others. You also tend to attract people who are positive, supportive and encourage your growth and development.

In contrast, low self-confidence can lead to a lack of self-esteem, self-doubt and negative self-talk, which can significantly impact your mental and emotional well-being. It can lead to a sense of helplessness, hopelessness and feeling stuck in life. It can also cause you to miss out on opportunities, and you may find it challenging to pursue your goals and ambitions.

Therefore, it is crucial to work on boosting your self-confidence in specific areas of your life. When you have self-confidence, you can enjoy a fulfilling and meaningful life, achieve your goals, and build positive relationships with others.

**When you have self-confidence, you are more likely to take risks, achieve your goals, and be happy with your life**

Self-confidence is a crucial factor in achieving success and happiness in life. When you have self-confidence, you are more likely to take risks, push past your comfort zone and pursue your goals and aspirations.

One of the primary reasons why self-confidence is so important is that it allows you to take risks. Many of the best opportunities in life require you to take a leap of faith, step outside of your comfort zone, and take a chance. When you have confidence in yourself and your abilities, you are more likely to take those risks and pursue those opportunities.

Having self-confidence also helps you to stay motivated and focused on achieving your goals. You believe that you are capable of achieving what you set out to do, and you are not easily deterred by setbacks or obstacles. This persistence and determination are essential ingredients for success in any area of your life.

When you achieve your goals, you experience a sense of accomplishment and satisfaction that contributes to your overall happiness and well-being. Setting goals and working towards them is an important part of personal growth and development, and self-confidence is essential in achieving those goals.

Moreover, self-confidence also helps to improve your mental and emotional well-being. When you have confidence in yourself, you feel more positive and optimistic about your life. You have a greater sense of self-worth, and you are less likely to be affected by negative thoughts or emotions.

On the other hand, low self-confidence can have a detrimental impact on your life. It can lead to self-doubt, negative self-talk and a lack of motivation to pursue your goals. This can cause you to miss out on opportunities and hinder your personal and professional growth.

Therefore, it is essential to work on building your self-confidence in specific areas of your life. By doing so, you are more likely to take risks, achieve your goals, and experience greater happiness and fulfillment. Building self-confidence takes time and effort, but the rewards are worth it.

## There are many things you can do to boost your self-confidence in specific areas

Building self-confidence is a process that requires effort and dedication, but it is achievable with the right strategies and techniques. There are many things you can do to boost your self-confidence in specific areas of your life, whether it be in your relationships, career, or personal life. Here are some effective strategies to help you build self-confidence in specific areas:

1. Identify your self-confidence blocks: One of the first steps in boosting your self-confidence is to identify the factors that are holding you back. These may include negative self-talk, fear of failure, or past experiences that have affected your self-esteem. By identifying these blocks, you can begin to work on overcoming them and building your self-confidence.

2. Challenge your negative thoughts: Negative self-talk can have a significant impact on your self-confidence. When you catch yourself thinking negatively, challenge those thoughts by asking yourself if they are rational and realistic. Replace those negative thoughts with positive affirmations that focus on your strengths and abilities.

3. Focus on your strengths: Recognize and celebrate your strengths, skills, and accomplishments. Focus on what

you are good at and find ways to use those strengths in specific areas of your life. When you have a positive view of your abilities, you are more likely to feel confident and capable.

4. Set realistic goals: Setting goals that are achievable and realistic can help you build self-confidence. Start with small, manageable goals and gradually work towards more significant accomplishments. Each time you achieve a goal, you will feel a sense of accomplishment and build confidence in your abilities.

5. Take risks: Taking risks and stepping outside of your comfort zone can help you build self-confidence in specific areas of your life. Whether it be trying something new or taking on a new challenge, the experience of facing your fears and overcoming obstacles can help you build self-confidence and resilience.

6. Surround yourself with positive people: The people you surround yourself with can have a significant impact on your self-confidence. Seek out relationships with positive, supportive people who encourage and inspire you to be your best self.

7. Practice positive self-talk: Positive self-talk can help you build self-confidence by shifting your focus to your strengths and abilities. Use positive affirmations and self-

talk to reinforce your confidence in yourself and your abilities.

In summary, building self-confidence in specific areas of your life requires effort and dedication, but it is achievable with the right strategies and techniques. By identifying your self-confidence blocks, challenging negative thoughts, focusing on your strengths, setting realistic goals, taking risks, surrounding yourself with positive people, and practicing positive self-talk, you can build self-confidence and achieve greater success and happiness in your life.

## Chapter 2: How to boost your self-confidence in specific areas

### Identify your self-confidence blocks

Identifying your self-confidence blocks is an essential step in boosting your self-confidence in specific areas. It involves understanding what is holding you back and preventing you from achieving your full potential. Self-confidence blocks can manifest in different ways and are often unique to each individual. In this section, we will discuss some of the common self-confidence blocks and strategies to overcome them.

1. Fear of failure

Fear of failure is one of the most common self-confidence blocks. Many people are afraid to take risks and try new things because they fear that they will fail. This fear can be paralyzing and prevent you from achieving your goals. To overcome this self-confidence block, it's essential to understand that failure is a natural part of the learning process. Every successful person has failed at some point in their lives. Instead of viewing failure as a negative outcome, see it as an opportunity to learn and grow. Embrace the mindset that failure is just feedback, and use it to make improvements and move forward.

2. Negative self-talk

Negative self-talk is another common self-confidence block. It involves the negative thoughts and beliefs that you have about yourself. Negative self-talk can be incredibly damaging to your self-confidence, as it reinforces limiting beliefs and prevents you from achieving your goals. To overcome this self-confidence block, it's essential to become aware of your negative self-talk and replace it with positive affirmations. Challenge your negative thoughts by asking yourself if they are true, and replace them with positive, empowering thoughts. For example, instead of saying, "I'm not good enough," say, "I am capable and deserving of success."

3. Comparing yourself to others

Comparing yourself to others is another common self-confidence block. It involves measuring your worth and success based on the achievements of others. This can be harmful to your self-confidence, as it leads to feelings of inadequacy and self-doubt. To overcome this self-confidence block, it's essential to focus on your own journey and progress. Recognize that everyone has their own unique path and that your journey is not comparable to anyone else's. Instead of comparing yourself to others, focus on your own goals and celebrate your accomplishments.

4. Perfectionism

Perfectionism is another common self-confidence block. It involves setting unrealistically high standards for yourself and being overly critical of your performance. This can be harmful to your self-confidence, as it leads to feelings of inadequacy and self-doubt. To overcome this self-confidence block, it's essential to embrace the mindset that done is better than perfect. Recognize that perfectionism is impossible, and striving for it will only hold you back. Instead, focus on progress and improvement, and celebrate your accomplishments along the way.

5. Lack of skills or knowledge

A lack of skills or knowledge is another common self-confidence block. It involves feeling inadequate because you lack the skills or knowledge to achieve your goals. This can be harmful to your self-confidence, as it reinforces limiting beliefs and prevents you from taking action. To overcome this self-confidence block, it's essential to recognize that skills and knowledge can be developed over time. Instead of feeling inadequate, focus on developing the skills and knowledge you need to achieve your goals. Take courses, read books, and seek out mentorship and guidance to help you develop the skills you need.

In conclusion, identifying your self-confidence blocks is an essential step in boosting your self-confidence in specific areas. By understanding what is holding you back and developing strategies to overcome these blocks, you can achieve your full potential and live a happy, successful life.

## Challenge your negative thoughts

One of the most significant barriers to self-confidence is negative self-talk. Negative thoughts can be extremely damaging and can lead to a lack of self-confidence, self-doubt, and even depression. It's essential to recognize these negative thoughts and challenge them. Here are some strategies that can help you challenge your negative thoughts and boost your self-confidence:

1. Identify your negative thoughts: The first step in challenging negative thoughts is to recognize them. Pay attention to the thoughts that run through your head when you're feeling down or anxious. Are you telling yourself that you're not good enough or that you'll never succeed? Write down these negative thoughts as they come to mind.

2. Question your negative thoughts: Once you've identified your negative thoughts, it's time to question them. Ask yourself if they're accurate or if there's evidence to support them. For example, if you're telling yourself that you're not good enough to get the promotion you want, ask yourself why you believe that. Is there any evidence to support that belief? Is it possible that you're just feeling insecure?

3. Reframe your negative thoughts: If you've identified a negative thought and found evidence that it's not

accurate, it's time to reframe it. Instead of telling yourself that you're not good enough to get the promotion, reframe the thought to something more positive. For example, you could tell yourself that you're qualified for the job and that you have a good chance of getting it.

4. Practice positive self-talk: Positive self-talk can be a powerful tool in boosting self-confidence. Start by creating a list of positive affirmations that you can say to yourself when you're feeling down or anxious. For example, you could tell yourself, "I am capable of achieving my goals," or "I am confident in my abilities." Repeat these affirmations to yourself regularly.

5. Focus on your strengths: When you're feeling down or lacking in self-confidence, it's easy to focus on your weaknesses. Instead, focus on your strengths. Make a list of your strengths and accomplishments and refer to it when you need a confidence boost. Celebrate your successes and remind yourself of your abilities.

6. Seek support: If you're struggling to challenge your negative thoughts on your own, seek support from friends, family, or a therapist. They can help you to see things from a different perspective and provide you with the encouragement and support you need to boost your self-confidence.

By challenging your negative thoughts, reframing them, and focusing on your strengths, you can overcome the self-doubt that's holding you back and boost your self-confidence. Remember, self-confidence is not something that comes naturally to everyone, but with practice and persistence, you can develop it and achieve your goals.

### Focus on your strengths

Focusing on your strengths is a crucial step in boosting your self-confidence in specific areas. It allows you to acknowledge your positive attributes and use them to overcome challenges and achieve success. Here are some ways to focus on your strengths and build self-confidence:

1. Identify your strengths: Start by making a list of your personal and professional strengths. Reflect on your experiences and accomplishments and identify the skills and qualities that helped you achieve them. If you have trouble identifying your strengths, ask a trusted friend or colleague for their input.

2. Use your strengths to set goals: Once you have identified your strengths, use them to set achievable goals. For example, if you are a great communicator, consider setting a goal to lead a presentation at work or to join a public speaking group.

3. Reframe your weaknesses: Instead of dwelling on your weaknesses, focus on your strengths and how they can help you overcome your weaknesses. For example, if you struggle with organization, focus on your problem-solving skills and ability to prioritize tasks.

4. Surround yourself with positivity: Spend time with people who uplift and support you. Surrounding yourself

with positive people can help you focus on your strengths and build your self-confidence.

5. Practice self-care: Taking care of yourself physically, emotionally, and mentally can help you feel more confident in your abilities. This can include getting enough sleep, eating well, exercising regularly, and practicing mindfulness or meditation.

6. Celebrate your successes: Celebrate your achievements, no matter how small they may seem. Recognizing your successes can help you feel more confident in your abilities and motivate you to keep working towards your goals.

By focusing on your strengths, reframing your weaknesses, surrounding yourself with positivity, practicing self-care, and celebrating your successes, you can build your self-confidence and achieve success in specific areas of your life.

## Set realistic goals

Setting realistic goals is an important step in boosting your self-confidence in specific areas of your life. When you set goals that are achievable, you can build momentum and confidence as you reach each milestone. Here are some tips for setting realistic goals that will help you build your self-confidence:

1. Identify your values and priorities: Before setting goals, it's important to have a clear understanding of what you value and prioritize in your life. Consider what is important to you in different areas of your life, such as your relationships, career, health, and personal growth. This will help you set goals that align with your values and priorities.

2. Use the SMART framework: The SMART framework is a popular goal-setting method that stands for Specific, Measurable, Achievable, Relevant, and Time-bound. When setting goals, make sure they are specific, measurable, achievable, relevant, and time-bound. For example, instead of setting a vague goal like "get healthier," set a specific goal like "exercise for 30 minutes a day, five days a week."

3. Break goals into smaller, manageable steps: When setting goals, break them into smaller, more manageable steps. This makes the goals less overwhelming and more

achievable. For example, if your goal is to write a book, break it into smaller steps like outlining the book, writing a chapter a week, and editing each chapter as you go.

4. Celebrate small wins: Celebrating small wins along the way can help boost your self-confidence and keep you motivated. When you achieve a small goal, take a moment to celebrate and acknowledge your progress.

5. Be flexible and adjust goals as needed: It's important to be flexible and adjust your goals as needed. Life is unpredictable, and sometimes circumstances change. Adjusting your goals as needed can help you stay on track and avoid feeling discouraged.

By setting realistic goals and breaking them into smaller steps, you can boost your self-confidence and achieve success in specific areas of your life. Remember to celebrate your progress along the way and be flexible as needed.

## Take risks

Taking risks can be intimidating, but it's an important step in boosting your self-confidence in specific areas. Here are some tips on how to take risks and step outside your comfort zone:

1. Identify your fear: What is holding you back from taking risks? Is it fear of failure, fear of rejection, or fear of the unknown? Once you identify your fear, you can work to overcome it.

2. Start small: Taking small risks can help build your confidence to take bigger ones. For example, if you're afraid of public speaking, start by speaking in front of a small group of friends or family members.

3. Prepare: Proper preparation can help alleviate some of the anxiety associated with taking risks. If you're preparing for a job interview, for example, research the company and practice your responses to common interview questions.

4. Visualize success: Visualizing yourself succeeding in your endeavors can help boost your confidence and reduce anxiety. Imagine yourself acing that job interview or giving a successful presentation.

5. Embrace failure: Failure is a natural part of taking risks. Don't let the fear of failure hold you back from trying

something new. Instead, view failure as an opportunity to learn and grow.

6. Seek support: Surround yourself with positive, supportive people who will encourage you to take risks and step outside your comfort zone.

7. Take action: Ultimately, the only way to build your confidence in taking risks is to take action. Start by setting small goals and gradually work your way up to bigger ones.

Remember, taking risks can be scary, but it's also an important step in boosting your self-confidence in specific areas. By identifying your fears, starting small, preparing, visualizing success, embracing failure, seeking support, and taking action, you can build the confidence to take on new challenges and achieve your goals.

## Surround yourself with positive people

Surrounding yourself with positive people is an effective way to boost your self-confidence. The people you spend time with can have a significant impact on your mindset, attitudes, and behaviors. If you surround yourself with positive, supportive individuals, you are more likely to feel good about yourself and your abilities. Here are some ways to surround yourself with positive people and boost your self-confidence:

1. Identify your positive influences: Take a look at the people in your life and think about who makes you feel good about yourself. These people could be family members, friends, colleagues, or mentors. Make a list of these positive influences and think about how you can spend more time with them.

2. Minimize time with negative people: Unfortunately, not everyone in your life will be a positive influence. There may be people who are critical, pessimistic, or unsupportive. While you may not be able to completely remove these people from your life, you can minimize your time with them. Limit your interactions with negative individuals, and focus on spending time with those who uplift and inspire you.

3. Join a supportive community: One way to surround yourself with positive people is to join a community or group that shares your interests or goals. Whether it's a sports team, a volunteer organization, or a professional association, being part of a community can provide you with a sense of belonging and support. Look for groups that align with your values and goals, and make an effort to participate regularly.

4. Seek out positive role models: Having positive role models can be a powerful way to boost your self-confidence. Look for people who have achieved success in areas that interest you, and study their habits and behaviors. This could be a mentor, a celebrity, or someone in your personal or professional network. Observe how they approach challenges, and try to emulate their positive mindset and outlook.

5. Practice positivity: Finally, to attract positive people into your life, it's important to practice positivity yourself. Focus on cultivating a positive mindset, and look for the good in every situation. Avoid negative self-talk, and instead, focus on your strengths and achievements. When you radiate positivity, you will naturally attract positive people into your life, and your self-confidence will soar.

## Practice positive self-talk

Positive self-talk is an essential tool for boosting self-confidence. It involves talking to yourself in a positive and encouraging manner, which can help to reframe negative thoughts and beliefs about yourself. Positive self-talk can help to boost your self-esteem, self-worth, and overall sense of well-being.

Here are some tips for practicing positive self-talk:

1. Be aware of your inner voice: The first step in practicing positive self-talk is to become aware of your inner voice. Pay attention to the things you say to yourself, especially when you're feeling down or insecure.

2. Challenge negative self-talk: Once you become aware of your negative self-talk, challenge it. Ask yourself if what you're saying is really true or if you're just being overly critical of yourself.

3. Reframe negative thoughts: When you catch yourself thinking negatively, reframe those thoughts in a more positive way. For example, if you find yourself thinking, "I'm never going to be good enough," reframe that thought to, "I'm working hard to improve, and I will get better with practice."

4. Use positive affirmations: Positive affirmations are a powerful tool for boosting self-confidence. These are short,

positive statements that you repeat to yourself throughout the day. Some examples include "I am confident and capable" and "I believe in myself and my abilities."

5. Celebrate your successes: Take time to celebrate your successes, no matter how small they may be. This can help to reinforce positive self-talk and build your self-confidence.

6. Practice gratitude: Gratitude is another powerful tool for boosting self-confidence. Take time each day to focus on the things you're grateful for in your life, and reflect on your own positive qualities and accomplishments.

7. Seek support: If you're struggling with negative self-talk, don't be afraid to seek support from friends, family, or a mental health professional. They can help you to reframe your thoughts and build your self-confidence.

In summary, positive self-talk is an important tool for boosting self-confidence. By challenging negative thoughts, reframing them in a more positive way, and using positive affirmations, you can build your self-esteem and sense of self-worth. Celebrating your successes, practicing gratitude, and seeking support can also help to reinforce positive self-talk and boost your overall confidence.

## Chapter 3: Boosting your self-confidence in your career

### Set career goals

Setting career goals is an important aspect of boosting self-confidence in your professional life. Goals give you direction, motivation, and a sense of accomplishment when achieved. Here are some tips on how to set career goals that will help you boost your self-confidence:

1. Define your career goals: Start by defining what you want to achieve in your career. This may include getting a promotion, starting your own business, or changing careers altogether. Write down your goals and make them as specific as possible.

2. Break down your goals: Once you have defined your career goals, break them down into smaller, more achievable tasks. This will help you create a roadmap to reach your goals and make them less daunting.

3. Make your goals SMART: SMART stands for specific, measurable, achievable, relevant, and time-bound. Make sure your career goals meet these criteria. For example, instead of setting a goal to "get a promotion," set a goal to "get promoted to manager within the next year by completing a leadership course and exceeding my sales targets."

4. Create an action plan: Once you have broken down your career goals into smaller tasks and made them SMART, create an action plan. This plan should include specific steps you need to take to achieve your goals, as well as a timeline for when you want to complete them.

5. Track your progress: Regularly track your progress toward your career goals. This will help you stay on track and make adjustments as needed. Celebrate your successes along the way, no matter how small they may be.

6. Seek feedback: Seek feedback from your manager, colleagues, or mentors on your progress toward your career goals. This can help you identify areas where you need to improve and give you a sense of what you are doing well.

Setting career goals is an important step in boosting your self-confidence in your professional life. By defining your goals, breaking them down into achievable tasks, making them SMART, creating an action plan, tracking your progress, and seeking feedback, you can increase your confidence in your abilities and achieve success in your career.

### Take on new challenges

Taking on new challenges can be a great way to boost your self-confidence in your career. When you step outside your comfort zone and try new things, you can gain a sense of accomplishment and feel more capable of taking on other challenges.

Here are some tips for taking on new challenges to boost your self-confidence in your career:

1. Volunteer for new projects: When a new project comes up at work, volunteer to be part of it. Even if it's outside your area of expertise, taking on a new project can help you learn new skills and gain experience.

2. Learn a new skill: If there's a skill you've always wanted to learn that would benefit your career, take the time to learn it. Whether it's a new software program or a new language, learning something new can help you feel more confident in your abilities.

3. Attend a conference or seminar: Attending a conference or seminar related to your field can be a great way to learn new things, meet new people, and gain confidence in your abilities.

4. Network: Meeting new people and building relationships can be a great way to boost your self-confidence in your career. Attend networking events, join

professional organizations, and connect with people on social media to expand your network.

5. Take on a leadership role: If there's an opportunity to take on a leadership role at work, consider taking it. Leading a team or project can help you gain confidence in your abilities and demonstrate your skills to others.

6. Take on more responsibility: If you feel comfortable with your current workload, consider taking on more responsibility. This can help you gain new skills and show your employer that you're capable of handling more complex tasks.

7. Seek feedback: Asking for feedback from your manager or colleagues can help you identify areas for improvement and gain confidence in your strengths. Use feedback to make adjustments and continue to grow in your career.

When taking on new challenges, it's important to remember that it's okay to make mistakes and experience setbacks. The most important thing is to learn from these experiences and continue to grow and develop your skills. By taking on new challenges and pushing yourself outside your comfort zone, you can boost your self-confidence in your career and achieve your goals.

### Network with other professionals

Networking is one of the most effective ways to boost your self-confidence in your career. Meeting and connecting with other professionals in your field can help you gain new insights, ideas, and opportunities, and can also help you build your reputation and credibility. Here are some tips on how to network effectively and boost your self-confidence in your career:

1. Attend industry events: One of the best ways to network with other professionals is to attend industry events such as conferences, trade shows, and seminars. These events provide opportunities to meet and connect with people who share your interests and expertise. Make sure to prepare ahead of time by researching the event and identifying people you want to meet.

2. Join professional associations: Joining a professional association can be a great way to network and connect with other professionals in your field. These associations often host events and conferences, and offer resources and support to help you advance in your career.

3. Participate in online forums: Online forums and groups can be a great way to connect with other professionals in your field, even if you are not able to attend

in-person events. Participate in discussions, share your ideas and expertise, and ask for advice and feedback.

4. Volunteer: Volunteering for industry events, conferences, or professional associations can be a great way to network with other professionals and gain new skills and experiences. It also shows your dedication and commitment to your field, which can help build your credibility and reputation.

5. Follow up: After meeting someone at an event or through networking, make sure to follow up with them to maintain the connection. Send a thank-you email or message, and keep in touch by sharing news and updates about your work.

Networking can be intimidating, especially if you are new to your field or are shy. However, with practice and persistence, you can become more comfortable and confident in your networking skills. Remember to be genuine, respectful, and professional in your interactions, and focus on building long-term relationships rather than just making a quick connection. By networking effectively, you can boost your self-confidence in your career and open up new opportunities for growth and success.

## Get involved in professional organizations

Getting involved in professional organizations is an excellent way to boost your self-confidence in your career. Professional organizations provide a platform for individuals to network, learn, and grow in their field. Here are some ways getting involved in professional organizations can help boost your self-confidence:

1. Access to resources and information

Professional organizations often provide their members with access to a wealth of resources and information, including industry-specific publications, research, and training materials. By taking advantage of these resources, you can enhance your knowledge and skills, which can boost your confidence in your abilities.

2. Opportunities for professional development

Many professional organizations offer workshops, conferences, and other training opportunities to their members. These events provide a chance to learn from experts in your field, develop new skills, and network with other professionals. Attending these events can help you build your confidence by giving you a sense of belonging to a community of like-minded individuals and by providing you with the tools you need to succeed.

3. Leadership opportunities

Getting involved in a professional organization can also provide opportunities to take on leadership roles, which can help you build your confidence and develop new skills. For example, you may have the opportunity to serve on a committee, lead a project, or even run for a position on the organization's board of directors. These experiences can help you develop your leadership abilities, build your network, and gain recognition within your field.

4. Networking opportunities

Professional organizations provide a platform for networking with other professionals in your field. This can help you build relationships with people who share your interests and goals, and who can offer advice, support, and mentorship. By expanding your network, you can gain exposure to new ideas and opportunities, and you can also build your confidence by knowing that you have a support system in place.

5. Recognition and awards

Many professional organizations offer awards and recognition programs to their members. By participating in these programs, you can gain recognition for your achievements and contributions to your field. This recognition can help boost your self-confidence by validating your skills and accomplishments and by demonstrating that others in your field value your work.

In conclusion, getting involved in professional organizations is an excellent way to boost your self-confidence in your career. By taking advantage of the resources, opportunities, and networking that these organizations offer, you can develop your skills, expand your knowledge, and build your confidence in your abilities.

### Dress for success

When it comes to boosting your self-confidence in your career, your appearance can play a big role. The way you present yourself can have a significant impact on how others perceive you, as well as how you feel about yourself. Dressing for success is an essential part of boosting your self-confidence and projecting a professional image in the workplace. In this section, we will discuss some tips on how to dress for success and boost your self-confidence in your career.

1. Dress Appropriately for Your Industry and Workplace

The first step in dressing for success is to understand the dress code of your industry and workplace. Different industries and workplaces have different expectations when it comes to professional attire. For example, a tech start-up might have a more casual dress code than a law firm. It's important to know what's appropriate and expected for your workplace and to dress accordingly. Dressing too casually or too formally can both send the wrong message and affect your self-confidence.

2. Invest in Quality Clothing

Investing in quality clothing can not only boost your self-confidence but also save you money in the long run.

High-quality clothing tends to last longer and require fewer replacements, which can ultimately save you money. Additionally, high-quality clothing tends to fit better, which can make you feel more confident and comfortable in your clothes. When shopping for professional attire, consider investing in pieces that are versatile, timeless, and well-made.

3. Pay Attention to Fit

Wearing clothes that fit well is crucial when it comes to boosting your self-confidence. Clothes that are too loose or too tight can make you feel uncomfortable and self-conscious. Take the time to try on clothes and find pieces that fit your body type well. Consider working with a tailor to make any necessary adjustments to ensure that your clothes fit you perfectly.

4. Accessorize Thoughtfully

Accessories can play an important role in your overall professional image. When choosing accessories, it's important to keep them simple and understated. Consider investing in high-quality, timeless pieces such as a classic watch or a leather bag. Avoid over-accessorizing, as it can be distracting and take away from your overall professional image.

5. Maintain Your Clothing

Maintaining your clothing is crucial when it comes to projecting a professional image and boosting your self-confidence. Make sure your clothes are clean, pressed, and free of any visible wear and tear. It's also important to take care of your shoes and other accessories, as they can impact your overall professional image.

### 6. Experiment with Color and Style

While it's important to dress appropriately for your industry and workplace, there's still room to experiment with color and style. Adding a pop of color or a unique accessory can help you stand out in a positive way and boost your self-confidence. However, it's important to balance this with the expectations of your industry and workplace.

### Conclusion

Dressing for success is an important part of boosting your self-confidence in your career. By understanding your industry and workplace's dress code, investing in quality clothing, paying attention to fit, accessorizing thoughtfully, maintaining your clothing, and experimenting with color and style, you can project a professional image and feel confident in your appearance. Remember, your appearance is just one part of your overall professional image, but it can have a significant impact on how you feel about yourself and how others perceive you.

### Be confident in your abilities

Being confident in your abilities is an essential aspect of professional success. It allows you to trust yourself and your skills, which in turn makes it easier for others to trust you. Confidence helps you to take on new challenges, make difficult decisions, and communicate effectively with others. However, building confidence in your abilities is not always easy. Here are some strategies to help you become more confident in your professional skills.

1. Know your strengths and weaknesses

Knowing your strengths and weaknesses is essential to building confidence in your abilities. It is important to recognize the areas where you excel and where you could improve. This self-awareness can help you focus on your strengths and build them up while also identifying areas where you need to grow. Consider taking a skills assessment test or asking for feedback from colleagues to gain a better understanding of your abilities.

2. Celebrate your successes

Celebrating your successes, no matter how small, can help you build confidence in your abilities. Take time to reflect on your achievements, recognize the hard work and effort that went into them, and celebrate your accomplishments. Recognizing your successes can help you focus on what you can do and give you the motivation to tackle new challenges.

3. Learn from failures

Failures are a natural part of professional growth. However, it is important to learn from them and not let them undermine your confidence. Take time to reflect on what went wrong and what you could do differently next time. Turn your failures into opportunities for growth and learning, and use them as a stepping stone to become even better in your field.

4. Seek out new challenges

Taking on new challenges is an excellent way to build confidence in your abilities. Look for opportunities to learn new skills, take on new responsibilities, or work on a project outside of your comfort zone. By stretching yourself, you will be able to develop new skills and gain experience, which will ultimately help you become more confident in your abilities.

5. Keep learning

Learning is a lifelong process, and staying up to date with the latest trends and developments in your field can help you build confidence in your abilities. Take courses, attend conferences, or read books and articles to stay current with your industry. This knowledge will help you feel more confident in your abilities and make you a more valuable asset to your organization.

6. Take care of yourself

Taking care of yourself is an essential part of building confidence in your abilities. Eat a healthy diet, exercise regularly, and get enough sleep. When you feel good physically, it can have a positive impact on your mental state and help you feel more confident in your abilities.

7. Visualize success

Visualization is a powerful tool that can help you build confidence in your abilities. Take time to visualize yourself succeeding in your career. Imagine yourself accomplishing your goals, receiving recognition for your hard work, and making a positive impact in your organization. By visualizing success, you can help build confidence in your abilities and give yourself the motivation to achieve your goals.

In conclusion, building confidence in your abilities is a critical aspect of professional success. By knowing your strengths and weaknesses, celebrating your successes, learning from your failures, seeking out new challenges, keeping learning, taking care of yourself, and visualizing success, you can become more confident in your abilities and achieve your career goals. Remember, confidence is not something that can be built overnight, but with consistent effort, you can become more self-assured and confident in your professional skills.

# Chapter 4: Boosting your self-confidence in your relationships

## Be yourself

Self-confidence is crucial for a healthy and fulfilling relationship. It helps you to be comfortable with who you are, which in turn makes it easier to build strong, authentic connections with others. Being yourself is one of the most important ways to build and maintain your self-confidence in relationships. In this section, we'll discuss the benefits of being yourself, and provide some tips for how to be more confident in expressing yourself.

Benefits of being yourself

When you are comfortable with who you are, you are more likely to attract people who accept and appreciate you for who you are. This can lead to more fulfilling relationships, where you feel comfortable being yourself and expressing your true thoughts and feelings.

Being authentic can also help you to avoid toxic or unhealthy relationships, as you are more likely to be able to identify and avoid people who don't accept you for who you are. It also helps you to build trust with others, as they can see that you are genuine and honest in your interactions.

Tips for being yourself

1. Embrace your strengths and weaknesses: We all have strengths and weaknesses, and accepting them is an important step towards building self-confidence. Embrace your strengths and work on improving your weaknesses. This will help you to feel more comfortable with who you are and will make it easier to express yourself.

2. Express your thoughts and feelings: It's important to express your thoughts and feelings, even if they are not popular or mainstream. Being honest and authentic about your thoughts and feelings helps you to connect with others on a deeper level. If you're not used to expressing yourself, start small by sharing your thoughts and feelings with someone you trust.

3. Accept compliments: Accepting compliments can be difficult for some people, but it's an important part of building self-confidence. When someone compliments you, accept it graciously, and avoid dismissing or downplaying the compliment. This will help you to build a more positive self-image.

4. Don't compare yourself to others: Comparing yourself to others can be damaging to your self-confidence. Everyone has their own unique strengths and weaknesses, and it's important to focus on your own strengths and

accomplishments. Instead of comparing yourself to others, focus on your own goals and progress.

5. Be honest about your needs: It's important to be honest about your needs and boundaries in a relationship. If you're not comfortable with something, express your discomfort in a respectful way. This will help you to build trust and respect with your partner, and will help you to feel more comfortable being yourself.

6. Practice self-care: Taking care of yourself is an important part of building self-confidence. Make sure to prioritize your own needs and take time to do things that make you feel good about yourself. This could include exercise, meditation, spending time with friends, or pursuing hobbies you enjoy.

Conclusion

Being yourself is an essential part of building self-confidence in your relationships. Embracing your strengths and weaknesses, expressing your thoughts and feelings, accepting compliments, avoiding comparisons, being honest about your needs, and practicing self-care are all important ways to build and maintain your self-confidence. By being comfortable with who you are, you can build more fulfilling relationships and lead a happier, more authentic life.

### Be honest and open with your partner

Being honest and open with your partner is a critical component of building and maintaining a healthy and strong relationship. However, it can also be challenging, especially if you struggle with self-confidence.

When you lack self-confidence, you may be afraid to express your thoughts and feelings to your partner. You may worry about their reaction or fear that they will reject you. However, keeping things bottled up can lead to resentment, misunderstandings, and a breakdown in communication.

Here are some tips for being honest and open with your partner while boosting your self-confidence:

1. Identify your fears: Start by identifying why you are hesitant to be honest and open with your partner. Are you afraid of rejection? Are you worried about their reaction? Understanding your fears can help you work through them and develop strategies for coping.

2. Practice self-compassion: Remember that it's okay to make mistakes and that everyone struggles with self-confidence at times. Be kind to yourself and treat yourself with the same compassion you would offer a friend.

3. Start small: If you're feeling overwhelmed, start by sharing small things with your partner. This could be something as simple as how your day was or something you

enjoyed doing. As you become more comfortable, you can start sharing more significant thoughts and feelings.

4. Choose the right time and place: It's important to choose the right time and place to have open and honest conversations with your partner. Avoid discussing important issues when you or your partner are tired, stressed, or distracted. Instead, choose a time when you both are relaxed and able to focus on each other.

5. Use "I" statements: When you are expressing your thoughts and feelings, use "I" statements instead of "you" statements. For example, say "I feel hurt when you do that," instead of "You always do that." This approach can help your partner understand your perspective and avoid triggering defensiveness.

6. Listen actively: Being honest and open with your partner is not just about expressing yourself; it's also about listening to your partner. Give your partner your full attention and show that you are actively listening by making eye contact, asking questions, and summarizing what they've said.

7. Accept your partner's response: Remember that your partner has their own thoughts and feelings, and they may not always respond in the way you want them to. Be

open to their response and avoid becoming defensive or critical.

Being honest and open with your partner is an essential part of building a healthy and strong relationship. By identifying your fears, practicing self-compassion, starting small, choosing the right time and place, using "I" statements, listening actively, and accepting your partner's response, you can boost your self-confidence and develop more meaningful and fulfilling relationships.

## Be supportive of your partner

Being supportive of your partner is essential in any healthy relationship. When you show support, you not only help your partner feel more confident and capable, but you also strengthen the bond between the two of you. Here are some ways to be supportive of your partner and boost your self-confidence in your relationship:

1. Listen actively One of the best ways to be supportive of your partner is to actively listen to them. Listen to what they have to say, validate their feelings, and ask questions to show that you care about their thoughts and opinions.

2. Offer encouragement Encouragement is a powerful tool to boost your partner's self-confidence. When your partner is feeling down, remind them of their strengths, encourage them to keep going, and remind them of their past successes.

3. Be there for them Being there for your partner in both good times and bad is important in any relationship. When your partner needs help or support, be there for them, even if it means putting your own needs aside for a while.

4. Celebrate their successes When your partner accomplishes something they're proud of, celebrate with them! Whether it's a small victory or a big milestone, take the time to acknowledge their success and share in their joy.

5. Show interest in their passions Another way to show support is to take an interest in your partner's passions and hobbies. Ask questions about what they enjoy, show interest in their work, and be supportive of their goals and dreams.

6. Be respectful Respect is a critical component of any healthy relationship. Treat your partner with kindness, respect their opinions, and avoid belittling or criticizing them.

7. Communicate openly Open communication is key to a successful relationship. Be honest with your partner about your thoughts, feelings, and needs, and encourage them to do the same.

8. Work as a team In any relationship, it's important to work together as a team. Whether you're facing a challenge or working towards a common goal, work together to achieve success.

9. Practice forgiveness Forgiveness is essential in any relationship, as we all make mistakes. When your partner makes a mistake, try to be understanding and forgiving. Similarly, when you make a mistake, take responsibility for your actions and seek forgiveness.

In conclusion, being supportive of your partner is crucial to building a healthy and happy relationship. By listening actively, offering encouragement, being there for them, celebrating their successes, showing interest in their passions, being respectful, communicating openly, working as a team, and practicing forgiveness, you can boost your self-confidence and strengthen your relationship.

### Spend quality time together

Spending quality time with your partner is an essential aspect of building a strong and healthy relationship. It's easy to get caught up in the hustle and bustle of daily life, but taking the time to prioritize your relationship can have a significant impact on boosting your self-confidence as well as strengthening the bond with your partner. In this section, we'll explore why spending quality time together is important and offer tips for making the most out of your time.

Why is spending quality time together important?

1. Reconnect with your partner: Spending time together allows you to reconnect with your partner and maintain a strong emotional connection. It provides an opportunity to share experiences, talk about your day, and listen to each other, which can help to deepen your bond.

2. Improve communication: Spending quality time together allows you to communicate more effectively with your partner. It provides an opportunity to talk openly and honestly about your feelings, concerns, and aspirations, which can help to strengthen your communication skills.

3. Reduce stress: Spending time with your partner can be a great way to relieve stress and unwind. Engaging in

enjoyable activities together can help you to forget about the stresses of work and life and enjoy each other's company.

Tips for spending quality time together:

1. Plan date nights: Schedule a regular date night to spend time together. It doesn't have to be anything fancy; it could be as simple as cooking dinner together or going for a walk in the park. The important thing is to make time for each other.

2. Try new things: Trying new activities together can be a fun and exciting way to spend time together. Whether it's trying a new restaurant or taking a dance class, exploring new experiences together can help to strengthen your bond and create lasting memories.

3. Unplug and disconnect: In today's digital age, it's easy to get distracted by screens and technology. Make a conscious effort to unplug and disconnect from technology during your quality time together. Focus on each other and the present moment.

4. Get outdoors: Spending time in nature can be a great way to reconnect with your partner and enjoy each other's company. Take a hike, go for a bike ride, or have a picnic in the park. Fresh air and physical activity can help to reduce stress and boost your mood.

5. Practice active listening: When spending quality time together, practice active listening. This means giving your full attention to your partner and truly listening to what they have to say. Avoid distractions and interruptions and make an effort to engage with your partner in meaningful conversation.

In conclusion, spending quality time with your partner is essential for building a strong and healthy relationship. It provides an opportunity to reconnect with each other, improve communication, and reduce stress. By following these tips and making an effort to prioritize your relationship, you can boost your self-confidence and strengthen your bond with your partner.

## Go on dates

Going on dates is an important part of any relationship. It allows you and your partner to spend quality time together, bond over shared experiences, and build a stronger connection. Going on dates also helps to break up the monotony of everyday life and inject some excitement and spontaneity into your relationship. Here are some tips on how to make the most out of your dates and boost your self-confidence in your relationship:

1. Plan the date together: When planning a date, make sure to involve your partner in the planning process. This allows both of you to have a say in what you do and can help to build excitement and anticipation for the date.

2. Try something new: Going on the same types of dates can become boring and predictable. To keep things interesting, try something new and out of your comfort zone. This can be anything from taking a cooking class together to going bungee jumping.

3. Dress up: Dressing up for a date can make you feel more confident and attractive. Choose an outfit that makes you feel good about yourself and shows off your personality.

4. Focus on the experience: Instead of worrying about whether or not your date likes you, focus on enjoying the experience and having fun. When you are fully engaged in

the moment, you are more likely to feel confident and relaxed.

5. Be present: Put away your phone and other distractions and be fully present with your partner. This shows that you value and respect them and can help to strengthen your connection.

6. Take turns planning the date: To keep things fresh and exciting, take turns planning the date. This allows both partners to have a say in what they want to do and can help to build a sense of adventure and spontaneity.

7. Be open-minded: Be open to trying new things and experiencing new things with your partner. This can help to build a stronger connection and make the relationship more exciting.

8. Communicate: Communication is key in any relationship, and it is especially important on a date. Be open and honest with your partner about your feelings, desires, and expectations for the date.

9. End the date on a positive note: End the date on a positive note by expressing your appreciation for your partner and the time you spent together. This can help to build a stronger connection and leave both partners feeling happy and fulfilled.

In conclusion, going on dates is an important part of any relationship. By planning the date together, trying something new, dressing up, focusing on the experience, being present, taking turns planning the date, being open-minded, communicating, and ending the date on a positive note, you can boost your self-confidence in your relationship and strengthen your connection with your partner.

## Make each other laugh

Having a good sense of humor is important in any relationship. Laughter can bring joy and happiness, and it can also help boost your self-confidence. When you and your partner are able to make each other laugh, it creates a positive atmosphere that can help you overcome any difficulties or challenges in your relationship.

Here are some ways to make each other laugh and boost your self-confidence in the process:

1. Share funny stories or memories: One way to make each other laugh is to share funny stories or memories from your past. This can be a great way to bond and connect with your partner, while also bringing some humor into your relationship.

2. Watch comedy shows or movies: Watching a funny movie or TV show together can be a great way to relax and have a good laugh. It can also provide some much-needed entertainment and distraction from the stresses of daily life.

3. Play games: Whether it's board games, card games, or video games, playing games together can be a fun way to bond and make each other laugh. Games that require some level of creativity or improvisation can be especially funny and entertaining.

4. Share jokes or memes: Sharing jokes or funny memes with each other can be a quick and easy way to make each other laugh. This can be especially helpful during stressful times, when you need a quick pick-me-up.

5. Be playful: Don't be afraid to be silly and playful with each other. This can involve teasing, tickling, or just goofing around. Being playful and lighthearted can help create a fun and positive atmosphere in your relationship.

6. Don't take yourselves too seriously: It's important to remember that everyone makes mistakes and nobody is perfect. Don't be too hard on yourself or your partner when things don't go as planned. Instead, try to find humor in the situation and laugh it off.

7. Celebrate milestones and achievements: Celebrating milestones and achievements together can be a great way to boost your self-confidence and make each other laugh. Whether it's a promotion at work, a successful project, or just reaching a personal goal, take the time to acknowledge and celebrate your accomplishments together.

In conclusion, making each other laugh is a great way to boost your self-confidence and strengthen your relationship. By sharing funny stories, watching comedy shows, playing games, sharing jokes and memes, being playful, not taking yourselves too seriously, and celebrating milestones and achievements together, you can create a positive and joyful atmosphere that will help you overcome any challenges in your relationship.

# Chapter 5: Boosting your self-confidence in your personal life

## Set personal goals

Setting personal goals is a crucial step in boosting your self-confidence in your personal life. It gives you direction, purpose, and a sense of accomplishment when you achieve those goals. In this section, we will discuss the importance of setting personal goals and how to do it effectively.

1. Why is setting personal goals important?

Setting personal goals is important for several reasons, including:

- It helps you focus: When you set personal goals, you know exactly what you want to achieve, and it helps you prioritize your efforts and time towards achieving them. This helps you avoid distractions and stay focused on your goals.

- It provides motivation: Setting personal goals can be motivating, as it gives you something to work towards. Achieving your goals gives you a sense of accomplishment, which can motivate you to set and achieve more goals.

- It boosts self-confidence: Accomplishing personal goals can boost your self-confidence and give you a sense of pride in your abilities.

- It improves self-awareness: Setting personal goals requires introspection and self-awareness. It helps you understand your strengths and weaknesses and identify areas where you need to improve.

2. How to set personal goals effectively

Setting personal goals can be overwhelming, but following these steps can help you set effective goals:

- Identify your priorities: Identify what is important to you and what you want to achieve. This will help you set goals that align with your values and priorities.

- Make your goals specific: Make your goals specific and measurable. This will help you track your progress and know when you have achieved your goal.

- Make your goals realistic: Set goals that are challenging but achievable. Setting unrealistic goals can be demotivating and lead to frustration.

- Set a deadline: Setting a deadline for your goals helps you stay focused and motivated.

- Break your goals down into smaller tasks: Breaking your goals down into smaller tasks makes them more manageable and less overwhelming.

- Write your goals down: Writing your goals down makes them more concrete and helps you remember them. It also serves as a reminder of what you are working towards.

3. Examples of personal goals

Here are some examples of personal goals you can set for yourself:

- Improve your physical fitness: Set a goal to exercise for a certain amount of time or number of days per week. You can also set a goal to run a 5k or participate in a fitness challenge.

- Learn a new skill: Set a goal to learn a new language, take a cooking class, or learn to play an instrument.

- Improve your mental health: Set a goal to practice mindfulness, meditate, or journal every day.

- Build better relationships: Set a goal to spend more quality time with loved ones, call or text friends more often, or join a social group.

- Focus on personal growth: Set a goal to read a certain number of books per month, attend personal development workshops, or start a gratitude journal.

4. Tips for achieving your personal goals

Here are some tips for achieving your personal goals:

- Stay motivated: Stay motivated by reminding yourself of why you set the goal in the first place. Celebrate small wins and progress along the way.

- Stay organized: Use a planner or calendar to keep track of your goals and progress.

- Get support: Surround yourself with supportive people who encourage and motivate you.

- Adjust your goals if needed: If you find that your goals are too challenging or not challenging enough, adjust them accordingly.

- Hold yourself accountable: Hold yourself accountable by tracking your progress and making adjustments if necessary.

In conclusion, setting personal goals is an essential step in boosting your self-confidence in your personal life. It helps you focus, motivates you, and boosts your self-confidence when you achieve those goals. By following these steps, you can set effective personal goals and achieve them.

## Take care of yourself

Taking care of oneself is a critical component of boosting self-confidence in one's personal life. It's essential to prioritize self-care as it not only helps in increasing self-esteem but also enhances overall well-being. In this section, we will discuss various ways to take care of oneself and boost self-confidence in one's personal life.

1. Prioritize Physical Health: A healthy mind resides in a healthy body. Therefore, it is essential to take care of one's physical health. Regular exercise, a nutritious diet, and proper sleep can go a long way in keeping you healthy and feeling good about yourself. Exercise releases endorphins, which are known as the "feel-good" hormones, and help reduce stress levels. Eating a balanced diet with plenty of fruits, vegetables, whole grains, and lean protein can help you feel energized and motivated. Getting enough restful sleep every night is also crucial for maintaining physical health.

2. Develop a Self-care Routine: Self-care is not just about getting enough sleep or eating well, but it also includes engaging in activities that make you feel happy and fulfilled. Engage in activities that bring you joy, such as reading, dancing, listening to music, or spending time with loved

ones. Incorporate these activities into your daily routine to ensure you make time for them regularly.

3. Practice Mindfulness: Mindfulness is the practice of being present and aware of one's thoughts and feelings without judgment. Practicing mindfulness can help you be more in tune with your emotions and improve your overall well-being. Mindfulness practices like meditation, yoga, and deep breathing exercises can help you become more self-aware and confident.

4. Take Time to Reflect: Reflecting on your accomplishments and progress can help you gain perspective and boost self-confidence. Reflecting on your past achievements can help you appreciate your strengths and capabilities. It is also a great way to identify areas where you need to improve and set personal goals for self-improvement.

5. Step Out of Your Comfort Zone: Doing things that are out of your comfort zone can help you overcome fear and build self-confidence. It can be as simple as trying a new hobby, taking up a new course or class, or traveling to a new place. Pushing yourself to do new things can help you build resilience and self-confidence.

6. Surround Yourself with Positive People: The people around you can have a significant impact on your self-

confidence. Surround yourself with people who encourage and support you. Being around positive people can help you build self-confidence and believe in your capabilities.

7. Embrace Failure: Failure is a part of life, and it's essential to embrace it. Every failure is an opportunity to learn and grow. Don't let fear of failure hold you back. Instead, view it as an opportunity to improve and do better next time. Embracing failure can help you build resilience and increase self-confidence.

In conclusion, self-care is essential for boosting self-confidence in one's personal life. Prioritizing physical health, developing a self-care routine, practicing mindfulness, reflecting on your progress, stepping out of your comfort zone, surrounding yourself with positive people, and embracing failure are some ways to take care of yourself and boost self-confidence in your personal life.

### Do things that make you happy

Doing things that make you happy is a key component of boosting your self-confidence in your personal life. When you engage in activities that bring you joy and fulfillment, you are more likely to feel positive and confident about yourself and your life. Here are some tips for doing things that make you happy and boosting your self-confidence in the process:

1. Make a list of activities you enjoy: Start by making a list of activities that bring you happiness and fulfillment. These can be anything from hiking and painting to cooking and reading. By identifying the activities that bring you joy, you can focus on doing more of them in your daily life.

2. Schedule time for your hobbies: Once you have identified the activities that make you happy, schedule time for them in your calendar. Whether it's an hour a day or a few hours a week, make sure you are setting aside dedicated time for the things that bring you joy.

3. Try new things: While it's important to focus on the activities you already enjoy, don't be afraid to try new things as well. Trying new activities can help you discover new passions and interests, which can in turn boost your self-confidence.

4. Surround yourself with positive people: When you are doing things that make you happy, surround yourself with people who are positive and supportive. Being around people who uplift and encourage you can make a big difference in how you feel about yourself.

5. Focus on the present moment: When you are engaging in activities that make you happy, try to be fully present in the moment. Don't worry about the past or the future, simply focus on enjoying the present moment and the activity you are engaged in.

6. Set achievable goals: If there is a particular activity that you are passionate about, set achievable goals for yourself to help you improve and grow in that area. For example, if you love painting, set a goal to paint a certain number of canvases by the end of the month.

7. Celebrate your successes: Finally, make sure to celebrate your successes along the way. When you achieve a goal or make progress in an area you are passionate about, take the time to acknowledge and celebrate your success. This will help you feel more confident and proud of your accomplishments.

In conclusion, doing things that make you happy is a great way to boost your self-confidence in your personal life. By focusing on activities that bring you joy, setting achievable goals, and celebrating your successes, you can cultivate a sense of happiness and fulfillment that will help you feel more positive and confident about yourself and your life.

### Spend time with loved ones

Spending time with loved ones is an essential part of boosting your self-confidence in your personal life. It can help you build stronger relationships, feel more connected, and create a support system that encourages you to be your best self. Whether it's family members, friends, or romantic partners, investing time and effort into these relationships can have a significant positive impact on your overall well-being.

Here are some ways to spend time with loved ones and boost your self-confidence:

1. Plan regular get-togethers: Set aside time each week or month to spend with your loved ones. It can be a simple dinner or a day trip to a nearby attraction. Regularly spending time together can help strengthen your relationships and give you something to look forward to.

2. Engage in shared activities: Participating in shared activities can help you create lasting memories and bond with your loved ones. This can be anything from playing board games or taking a cooking class to going on a hiking trip or volunteering for a cause you all care about.

3. Have meaningful conversations: Take the time to have meaningful conversations with your loved ones. Talk about your goals, dreams, and struggles. By sharing your

experiences and supporting each other, you can build deeper connections and feel more confident in your relationships.

4. Practice active listening: When you spend time with loved ones, make an effort to actively listen to what they have to say. Avoid distractions like your phone or TV and engage in the conversation. This can help you better understand your loved ones and make them feel valued and heard.

5. Create new traditions: Creating new traditions can help you build stronger bonds with your loved ones and give you something to look forward to. This can be anything from an annual holiday gathering to a weekly game night. By sharing experiences and creating new memories, you can strengthen your relationships and boost your self-confidence.

6. Show appreciation: Take the time to show your loved ones how much you appreciate them. Express gratitude for their support and love, and acknowledge their positive impact on your life. This can help create a positive cycle of support and confidence, making you feel more confident and loved.

7. Embrace differences: Everyone is different, and that's okay. Embrace the differences between you and your loved ones, and celebrate what makes each of you unique. By

accepting each other's differences, you can build stronger relationships and create a sense of belonging and acceptance.

In conclusion, spending time with loved ones is an important part of boosting your self-confidence in your personal life. By engaging in shared activities, having meaningful conversations, and showing appreciation, you can create deeper connections with your loved ones and feel more confident and supported.

## Give back to others

Giving back to others is an incredibly rewarding experience that can boost your self-confidence and overall happiness. When you help others, you feel good about yourself and your ability to make a difference in the world. In this section, we'll explore the different ways you can give back to others and improve your own self-confidence in the process.

1. Volunteer your time

One of the easiest and most fulfilling ways to give back to others is by volunteering your time. There are countless organizations and causes that are always in need of volunteers, and finding one that aligns with your interests and passions is a great way to start. Whether you're helping out at a local soup kitchen, mentoring young students, or assisting with a community clean-up, volunteering your time can provide a sense of purpose and fulfillment that can boost your self-confidence.

2. Donate to charity

If you're unable to volunteer your time, another way to give back to others is by donating to charity. There are countless organizations that rely on donations to fund their important work, and even a small donation can make a big difference. Whether you choose to donate to a local charity or a larger organization that aligns with your values, giving back in this way can provide a sense of fulfillment and purpose.

3. Spread kindness

Small acts of kindness can make a big impact in the lives of others, and can also boost your own self-confidence. Whether it's holding the door open for someone, giving a compliment, or simply smiling and saying hello, spreading kindness can make you feel good about yourself and your ability to make a positive impact in the world.

4. Mentor someone

If you have skills or knowledge in a particular area, consider mentoring someone who is just starting out. Whether it's a younger sibling, a neighbor, or a student in your community, sharing your expertise and experience can provide a sense of fulfillment and purpose. Mentoring someone can also be a great way to build your own self-confidence and strengthen your own skills.

5. Support a cause

Whether it's a local cause or a national movement, supporting a cause that aligns with your values can provide a sense of purpose and fulfillment. Whether you're attending a protest, signing a petition, or simply sharing information about the cause on social media, supporting a cause can be a great way to boost your own self-confidence and feel like you're making a difference in the world.

6. Give back to your community

Giving back to your community can take many forms, whether it's through volunteering, donating, or simply being a good neighbor. By taking an active role in your community, you can build connections with others and feel like you're making a positive impact. This can boost your self-confidence and make you feel like a valued member of your community.

In conclusion, giving back to others is a great way to boost your self-confidence and overall happiness. Whether it's through volunteering your time, donating to charity, spreading kindness, mentoring someone, supporting a cause, or giving back to your community, there are countless ways to make a positive impact in the world. By giving back, you can feel good about yourself and your ability to make a difference in the lives of others.

### Be grateful for what you have

Being grateful is an essential aspect of building self-confidence and improving our well-being. It is easy to focus on the things that we lack, but practicing gratitude can shift our attention to the positive aspects of our lives. When we recognize and appreciate what we have, we develop a positive mindset that can enhance our self-confidence and overall satisfaction. In this section, we will discuss the benefits of practicing gratitude and ways to cultivate it in our lives.

Benefits of Gratitude

Gratitude can bring a multitude of benefits to our lives. Here are some of the ways that gratitude can help boost our self-confidence:

1. Increases happiness: Practicing gratitude can help us focus on the positive aspects of our lives, leading to a happier and more fulfilling life.

2. Improves relationships: Expressing gratitude towards others can strengthen our relationships and foster a sense of connection and appreciation.

3. Reduces stress: Gratitude can help reduce stress levels and increase our resilience to challenges, leading to better mental and physical health.

4. Enhances empathy: Practicing gratitude can improve our ability to empathize with others, leading to more meaningful and positive relationships.

Ways to Practice Gratitude

1. Keep a gratitude journal: Writing down what we are grateful for each day can help us focus on the positive aspects of our lives. Take a few minutes each day to jot down things that you appreciate, whether it be a good cup of coffee or a loving friend.

2. Express gratitude to others: Take time to express your gratitude to those around you. A simple thank you note or verbal expression of gratitude can go a long way in strengthening relationships and fostering positivity.

3. Practice mindfulness: Mindfulness is the practice of being present and aware of our thoughts and feelings. By being mindful, we can cultivate an attitude of gratitude and focus on the positive aspects of our lives.

4. Volunteer or give back: Volunteering or donating to charity is an excellent way to show gratitude and appreciation for what we have. It can also enhance our sense of purpose and well-being.

5. Practice positive self-talk: Practicing positive self-talk and focusing on our strengths and accomplishments can

help us develop a sense of gratitude for ourselves and the things we have achieved.

Incorporating gratitude into our daily lives can have significant positive effects on our self-confidence and overall well-being. By focusing on the positive aspects of our lives and showing gratitude towards ourselves and others, we can develop a sense of appreciation and satisfaction that can enhance our confidence and happiness.

## Conclusion
## The importance of boosting your self-confidence in specific areas

Self-confidence is a vital component of our overall well-being and success in life. In this book, we have explored various ways in which we can boost our self-confidence in different areas of our lives, such as career, relationships, and personal life. It is important to recognize that each area of our lives has unique challenges and opportunities for growth, and developing self-confidence in these areas can have a profound impact on our overall sense of self-worth and happiness.

Boosting your self-confidence in your career can lead to increased job satisfaction, better job performance, and greater opportunities for advancement. By setting career goals, taking on new challenges, networking with other professionals, dressing for success, and being confident in your abilities, you can become a more valuable and effective employee.

Boosting your self-confidence in your relationships can lead to deeper and more fulfilling connections with loved ones. By being yourself, honest, and open with your partner, supportive, spending quality time together, going on dates, and making each other laugh, you can build stronger and more resilient relationships that bring joy and happiness into your life.

Boosting your self-confidence in your personal life can lead to greater personal fulfillment and life satisfaction. By setting personal goals, taking care of yourself, doing things that make you happy, spending time with loved ones, giving back to others, and being grateful for what you have, you can build a sense of purpose and meaning in your life that transcends any setbacks or challenges you may face.

It is important to recognize that boosting your self-confidence is not a one-time event, but rather an ongoing process that requires commitment and dedication. It may involve stepping outside of your comfort zone, facing your fears, and taking risks. However, the rewards of increased self-confidence are immeasurable, and can lead to a life filled with greater joy, success, and fulfillment.

In conclusion, the importance of boosting your self-confidence in specific areas of your life cannot be overstated. By focusing on your strengths, setting goals, taking on new challenges, building strong relationships, and taking care of yourself, you can achieve greater levels of success and happiness than you ever thought possible. It is my hope that the strategies and tips provided in this book will serve as a roadmap to help you boost your self-confidence and achieve your goals in life. Remember, with self-confidence, anything is possible!

## How to boost your self-confidence in specific areas

In this chapter, we have explored various strategies to boost self-confidence in different areas of life, including career, relationships, and personal life. In this section, we will summarize these strategies and provide additional tips on how to implement them in your life.

Boosting self-confidence in your career:

1. Identify your strengths and weaknesses: Start by identifying your strengths and weaknesses. This will help you to focus on your strengths and work on your weaknesses.

2. Take on new challenges: Challenge yourself to take on new tasks and responsibilities. This will help you to develop new skills and knowledge, and boost your confidence.

3. Network with other professionals: Build relationships with other professionals in your industry. This will help you to learn from their experiences and gain insights into your field.

4. Get involved in professional organizations: Join professional organizations related to your field. This will help you to stay up-to-date on industry trends and connect with other professionals.

5. Dress for success: Dress professionally and appropriately for your industry. This will help you to project a confident image and feel more confident in yourself.

6. Be confident in your abilities: Believe in yourself and your abilities. Don't let self-doubt hold you back from pursuing your goals.

Boosting self-confidence in your relationships:

1. Be yourself: Be true to yourself and don't try to be someone you're not. This will help you to feel more comfortable and confident in your relationships.

2. Be honest and open with your partner: Communicate openly and honestly with your partner. This will help you to build trust and strengthen your relationship.

3. Be supportive of your partner: Support your partner's goals and dreams. This will help them to feel valued and supported, and strengthen your relationship.

4. Spend quality time together: Make time to spend quality time with your partner. This will help you to build a stronger connection and deepen your relationship.

5. Go on dates: Plan regular dates with your partner. This will help you to keep the romance alive and maintain a strong connection.

6. Make each other laugh: Share your sense of humor with your partner. Laughing together can help to reduce stress and increase feelings of closeness.

Boosting self-confidence in your personal life:

1. Set personal goals: Set goals for yourself and work towards achieving them. This will help you to feel a sense of accomplishment and boost your self-confidence.

2. Take care of yourself: Practice self-care by taking care of your physical, emotional, and mental health. This will help you to feel more confident and in control of your life.

3. Do things that make you happy: Make time for activities that bring you joy and happiness. This will help you to feel more fulfilled and satisfied in your life.

4. Spend time with loved ones: Connect with family and friends who support and encourage you. This will help you to feel loved and valued.

5. Give back to others: Volunteer your time and talents to help others. This will help you to feel more connected to your community and make a positive impact on the world.

6. Be grateful for what you have: Focus on what you have rather than what you don't have. Gratitude can help to increase feelings of happiness and contentment.

In conclusion, self-confidence is a key ingredient for success in all areas of life. By focusing on your strengths, taking on new challenges, building relationships, practicing self-care, and being grateful, you can boost your self-confidence and achieve your goals. Remember, boosting self-confidence is a process that takes time and effort, but the rewards are well worth it.

**THE END**

## Wordbook

Welcome to the glossary section of this book. Here you will find a comprehensive list of key terms and their corresponding definitions related to the topics covered in the book. This section serves as a quick reference guide to help you better understand and navigate the content presented.

1. Self-confidence: The belief in oneself and one's abilities or qualities.

2. Self-esteem: The subjective evaluation of one's worth or value as a person.

3. Self-talk: The internal dialogue that occurs in a person's mind, which can either be positive or negative.

4. Self-image: The mental and physical picture one has of oneself, which can affect one's self-confidence.

5. Mindfulness: The practice of being present in the moment, without judgment or distraction, which can help improve self-confidence.

6. Positive affirmations: Positive statements or beliefs that can help counter negative self-talk and boost self-confidence.

7. Resilience: The ability to bounce back from setbacks or challenges, which can improve self-confidence.

8. Assertiveness: The ability to express oneself confidently and respectfully, which can improve self-confidence in interpersonal relationships.

9. Self-care: The practice of taking care of oneself physically, emotionally, and mentally, which can improve self-confidence.

10. Self-compassion: The practice of treating oneself with kindness, care, and understanding, which can improve self-confidence and self-esteem.

## Supplementary Materials

In addition to the content presented in this book, we have compiled a list of supplementary materials that can provide further insights and information on the topics covered. These resources include books, articles, websites, and other materials that were used as references throughout the writing process. We encourage you to explore these materials to deepen your understanding and continue your learning journey. Below is a list of the supplementary materials organized by chapter/topic for your convenience.

Introduction

- Bandura, A. (1977). Self-efficacy: Toward a unifying theory of behavioral change. Psychological Review, 84(2), 191-215.
- Neff, K. D. (2011). Self-compassion, self-esteem, and well-being. Social and Personality Psychology Compass, 5(1), 1-12.

Chapter 1

- Deci, E. L., & Ryan, R. M. (2008). Self-determination theory: A macrotheory of human motivation, development, and health. Canadian Psychology/Psychologie Canadienne, 49(3), 182-185.
- Rosenberg, M. (1965). Society and the adolescent self-image. Princeton University Press.

Chapter 2

- Albert Bandura (1994). Self-efficacy. In V. S. Ramachaudran (Ed.), Encyclopedia of human behavior (Vol. 4, pp. 71-81). Academic Press.
- Feltz, D. L., & Lirgg, C. D. (2001). Self-efficacy beliefs of athletes, teams, and coaches. Handbook of sport psychology, 2, 340-361.

Chapter 3

- Hargreaves, A. (2000). Mixed emotions and teacher identity: A post-structural perspective. Teachers and teaching, 6(1), 31-47.
- Judge, T. A., & Bono, J. E. (2001). Relationship of core self-evaluations traits--self-esteem, generalized self-efficacy, locus of control, and emotional stability--with job satisfaction and job performance: A meta-analysis. Journal of applied psychology, 86(1), 80.

Chapter 4

- Collins, N. L., & Feeney, B. C. (2000). A safe haven: An attachment theory perspective on support seeking and caregiving in intimate relationships. Journal of personality and social psychology, 78(6), 1053.
- Reis, H. T., & Shaver, P. (1988). Intimacy as an interpersonal process. Handbook of personal relationships: Theory, research and interventions, 367-389.

Chapter 5

- Diener, E., Suh, E. M., Lucas, R. E., & Smith, H. L. (1999). Subjective well-being: Three decades of progress. Psychological bulletin, 125(2), 276.

- Fredrickson, B. L. (2004). Gratitude, like other positive emotions, broadens and builds. The psychology of gratitude, 145-166.

Conclusion

- Baumeister, R. F., Campbell, J. D., Krueger, J. I., & Vohs, K. D. (2003). Does high self-esteem cause better performance, interpersonal success, happiness, or healthier lifestyles?. Psychological Science in the Public Interest, 4(1), 1-44.

- Neff, K. D. (2016). The self-compassion scale is a valid and theoretically coherent measure of self-compassion. Mindfulness, 7(1), 264-274.

www.ingramcontent.com/pod-product-compliance
Lightning Source LLC
LaVergne TN
LVHW010403070526
838199LV00065B/5886